THE HIDDEN SECRET TO SUCCESS

Be your own boss

By Onyema Uche Chigozie

Table of contents

HOW TO KEEP/MAINTAIN SUCCESS

HOW TIME AFFECT SUCCESS

INTRODUCTION

The secret to success is your success guide book, it is packed with proven, tested and experienced strategies, points and insights to guide you on your daily activities, desire and need to achieve and maintain success.

SUCCESS IN FULL MEANING

1.

Success can mean different things to different people. It could mean achieving a goal, such as a financial milestone or an athletic accomplishment, or it could involve personal growth and development. Whatever success means to an individual, it is typically achieved by setting a goal, taking action to reach that goal, and then reflecting on the outcome.

When striving for success, it is important to set goals that are meaningful and achievable. This requires taking the time to reflect on what is important to you and what you want to achieve. Once you have a goal in mind, it is important to create a plan of action to reach that goal. This plan should include both short-term and long-term steps, and should be realistic and achievable.

In order to stay motivated and on track, it is important to set up rewards for yourself along the way. This could involve taking a break for a day or having a treat when you reach a certain milestone. Additionally, it is important to track your progress and to celebrate your successes.

Success is not only achieved through hard work, but also through resilience and determination. It is important to remember that it is okay to make mistakes or take a break, as long as you continue to strive towards your goal. This means learning from your mistakes and using them as a way to improve and grow.

Finally, success is often achieved by staying positive, believing in yourself, and having a good support system. Surrounding yourself with people who believe in you and are encouraging can help you to stay motivated and reach your goals.

No matter what success means to you, it involves setting a goal, creating a plan, and taking action. It is about learning and growing, and believing in yourself. Success is achievable, and with hard work, determination, and resilience, you can reach your goals.

2.

Success is a feeling of personal accomplishment and satisfaction. It is the favorable outcome of an effort or task that has been pursued with dedication and determination. It is a positive state of mind that is the result of successfully reaching a goal or achieving an objective.

Success is often seen as a process rather than an end goal. It is a journey that involves hard work, dedication, and perseverance. Along the way, there will be obstacles and setbacks, but with a clear focus and strong commitment, success is achievable.

Success requires planning and a detailed roadmap. It requires analyzing and assessing the situation, setting realistic goals, and creating a plan of action to reach those goals. It involves setting short-term and long-term goals and taking action to achieve them. It also requires taking risks, learning from failures, and continuously improving and adapting.

Success also requires the development of certain skills, such as communication, problem-solving, and decision-making. It involves being able to work well with others and having a positive attitude and mindset.

Successful people also have the ability to stay focused and motivated. They have the ability to stay positive and resilient in the face of adversity. They are able to stay organized and manage their time effectively.

Finally, successful people are able to recognize the importance of balance and self-care. They understand that their physical and mental health are important and take the necessary steps to ensure their well-being.

Success is a journey that requires hard work, dedication, and perseverance. With a clear focus and strong commitment, success is achievable. With the right skills and mindset, success can be achieved with balance and self-care.

3.

Success can mean many different things to different people; it is a very personal and subjective concept. However, success is often thought of as achieving a goal or target, whether it is financial, professional, or personal. It can also be thought of as a feeling of satisfaction and happiness that comes from having achieved something.

Success involves setting goals and striving to meet them. It may also involve making changes to achieve the desired outcome. It requires setting realistic goals, and taking actionable steps to reach them. Having a plan and a timeline to follow can help to keep one on track and motivated. It is important to keep in mind that success can take many forms, and it doesn't have to be financial or career-related. It could be a personal goal such as learning a new skill, losing weight, or completing a project.

In order to be successful, it is important to have a positive mindset and to focus on the end goal. Having a positive attitude and being open to failure can help to keep one motivated. It is also important to stay organized and have a plan for the steps that need to be taken to reach the desired result.

Success can also involve taking risks, as well as learning from mistakes. Taking risks can help to create opportunities for growth and development. Taking the time to reflect on successes and failures can help to learn from mistakes, and also to recognize and appreciate the wins.

In a nutshell, success is a personal concept that involves setting and meeting goals, having a positive attitude, taking risks and learning from mistakes, and having the motivation to keep pushing forward. It is important to remember that success is a journey and that it looks different for everyone.

4.

Success is the accomplishment of an aim or purpose. It is the achievement of something desired, planned, or attempted. Achieving success involves setting goals and working hard to reach them. Goals should be realistic, measurable, attainable, and timely.

Success is often a result of dedication and perseverance. It requires sustained effort, motivation, and a positive attitude. People who are successful often have a clear sense of purpose, good problem-solving skills, and excellent communication and interpersonal skills. They also have the ability to stay focused, even when faced with obstacles.

Successful people tend to have a strong work ethic and are persistent in the face of adversity. They are creative, innovative, and willing to take risks. They are also able to learn from their mistakes and move forward.

Successful people also have a supportive network of family, friends, and colleagues. These people provide encouragement and help to make dreams come true. Having a strong support system is essential for reaching goals.

Success is most often associated with money, power, and status. It is important to remember, however, that success can be achieved in many other areas. It can be achieved in relationships, health, education, career, and personal development.

Ultimately, success is determined by individual beliefs and values. It is a personal journey and journey of growth. To be successful, one must be open to learning, willing to take risks, and have an optimistic outlook. With dedication, hard work, and determination, success is achievable.

STEPS TO ACHIEVING SUCCESS

1.

Achieving success is an important goal for many people, but it isn't always easy. Success requires hard work, dedication, and perseverance. To achieve success, it's important to focus on the steps that will lead you to your desired outcome.

The first step is to set a goal. Setting a goal will allow you to focus your energy and efforts on what you want to accomplish.

Break down your goal into smaller, achievable steps, and set deadlines for each step. This will help you stay on track and motivated.

The second step is to take action. Once you have your goal and plan in place, it's time to take action. This may mean making phone calls, attending meetings, or doing research. Take action every day, no matter how small, towards achieving your goal.

The third step is to be persistent. Success is rarely achieved overnight, so don't give up if you don't see results right away. Keep working hard and stay focused on your goal. Don't be afraid to make mistakes, as it's often through trial and error that you eventually find success.

The fourth step is to stay positive. Having a positive attitude and outlook is key when it comes to achievingsuccess.You'llface many challenges along the way, so it's important to stay focused on the end goal and remain hopeful.

The fifth step is to ask for help. No one can do it all alone, so don't be afraid to ask for help. Find mentors or people who have achieved success in the same area to help you. They can provide valuable advice that will help you reach your goals.

These are the five steps to achieving success. Remember to set a goal, take action, be persistent, stay positive, and ask for help. Follow these steps and you'll be well on your way to achieving your desired outcome.

2.

Achieving success is a process that requires dedication, focus, and patience. The steps of achieving success can vary depending on the individual and the goal they are trying to accomplish, but there are some basic steps that are universal.

First and foremost, it is important to have a clear goal in mind.

Without a goal, it is impossible to determine what success looks like and how to get there. Make sure to have a specific goal and plan, and write it down so it can be referred to often and adjusted as needed.

Once a goal is established, it is important to break it down into smaller, achievable steps. This will make it easier to take action and will help keep momentum going. Setting short-term goals and celebrating each accomplishment will help provide motivation and a sense of satisfaction.

In addition to having a plan, it is important to have the right attitude and mindset. A positive attitude will help you stay focused and motivated, while a negative attitude will make even the smallest tasks feel insurmountable. It is important to stay focused on the end goal, and to not become too discouraged by setbacks or failures.

It is also important to stay organized and be mindful of time management. This means setting deadlines and sticking to them, as well as prioritizing tasks. Make sure to be realistic with the amount of time needed to finish tasks and not overextend yourself.

Finally, it is important to remember to take care of yourself. Success requires hard work and dedication, but it is also important to take time for yourself to relax and recharge. Achieving success can be a long and exhausting process, and taking regular breaks can help keep motivation and morale high.

By following these steps, you can set yourself on a path to success. Having a clear goal, breaking it down into achievable steps, having the right attitude, staying organized and mindful of time, and taking care of yourself are all essential elements in achieving success. With dedication and hard work, success can be yours.

3.

To achieve success you must understand that Success is an ambitious and admirable goal to strive for. It can be achieved through hard work and dedication, as well as a few key steps.

The first step in achieving success is to set clear, achievable goals. Without targets to reach, it can be difficult to stay motivated and make progress. It is important to set realistic goals, as well as long-term and short-term goals. This will help to break down the long-term goals into achievable tasks, and will give you something to work towards.

The second step is to develop a plan and stay organized. Having a plan with an achievable timeline will help to keep you on track and motivated. It is also important to stay organized, as this will make it easier to complete tasks efficiently.

The third step is to stay motivated and focused. Noting progress, no matter how small, will help to keep you focused and motivated. It is also important to recognize any obstacles that may arise, and to have strategies in place to overcome them.

The fourth step is to stay persistent and consistent. Success doesn't happen overnight, and it is important to stay consistent in order to make progress. It is also important to stay persistent, even when progress is slow, as this will help to maintain motivation.

The fifth step is to stay positive and open to learning. The more you learn, the more successful you will be. It is also important to stay positive, as this will help to maintain motivation and enthusiasm.

Finally, the sixth step is to reflect and adjust. Reflecting on your progress and successes, as well as any mistakes you may have made, will help to inform future decisions and strategies. It is also important to make adjustments to your plans and strategies, as this will help to ensure that you reach your goals.

Success is an achievable goal, and by following these steps, you can reach it. Through setting realistic goals, staying organized, staying motivated and focused, staying persistent and consistent, staying positive and open to learning, and reflecting and adjusting, you can achieve success.

POSSIBLE THINGS THAT CAN DELAY SUCCESS

1.

Success is a desired outcome for many people, but it can be hindered by various factors. One of the most common things that can delay success is a lack of motivation. Without motivation, it can be difficult to stay on track and make progress towards achieving your goals. Additionally, procrastination can be a major roadblock to success. When we procrastinate, we put off tasks that we should be completing, which can leave us feeling overwhelmed and behind. Another factor that can delay success is fear. Fear of failure or fear of the unknown can prevent us from taking risks and trying new things that could potentially lead to success.

Another possible thing that can delay success is a lack of resources. Without access to the right resources, it can be difficult to accomplish our goals. This could include a lack of financial resources, access to education, or access to mentors and advisors.

Finally, inadequate time management skills can be a major obstacle to success. Poor time management can lead to missed deadlines, incomplete projects, and inefficient work habits.

Overall, there are many possible things that can delay success. From a lack of motivation, procrastination, fear, lack of resources, and inadequate time management skills, these can all be major roadblocks to achieving our desired goals. Understanding the factors that can delay success can help us develop strategies to mitigate these issues and increase our chances of success.

2.

Success can be a complex concept, and there are many potential things that can delay its achievement. A few of the most common factors that can delay success are:

1. Lack of Preparation: When you don't take the time to adequately research and plan, you can set yourself up for failure. Proper preparation is essential for success, especially when it comes to complex tasks. Taking shortcuts or cutting corners can lead to

mistakes and delays in achieving success.

2. Poor Time Management: Poor time management can have a direct impact on success. Not taking the time to plan and prioritize tasks can lead to missed deadlines and cause delays.

3. Procrastination: Procrastination is a major roadblock to success. Those who procrastinate often find themselves feeling overwhelmed and unable to complete tasks in a timely manner.

4. Fear of Failure: Fear of failure can be paralyzing and it can cause delays in progress. It is important to recognize and address any anxiety or fear that you may be feeling in order to move forward and achieve success.

5. Lack of Focus: Having too many goals and tasks can be detrimental to success. It is important to focus on a few key goals in order to maximize your chances of success.

6. Lack of Motivation: When you are not motivated or inspired, it can be difficult to stay on track and make progress. You need to be motivated to stay focused and be proactive in order to achieve success.

These are just a few of the possible things that can delay success. With proper planning, time management, focus, and motivation, you can set yourself up for success and avoid any potential delays.

3.

Success is a subjective term, as what constitutes success varies from person to person. However, there are certain things that can delay the success of an individual or organization. One of the most common reasons for a delay in success is a lack of planning. For example, if an individual does not take the time to plan out their goals and objectives, they may find themselves struggling to make progress which can lead to delays in success.

Another possible thing that could delay success is a lack of resources. If an individual or organization does not have the necessary resources to accomplish their goals, it can be difficult to make progress and ultimately reach success. This can be especially true if the resources needed are expensive or hard to come by.

In some cases, a lack of motivation can also be a factor in delaying success. If an individual or organization does not have the drive to put in the hard work and dedication necessary to achieve success, it can be difficult for them to make progress.

Finally, an individual or organization may experience a delay in success if they lack the necessary skills or knowledge to accomplish their goals. If an individual or organization does not have the right skills or knowledge to accomplish their objectives, they may struggle to make progress and ultimately reach success.

In conclusion, there are several possible things that can delay success. These include a lack of planning, a lack of resources, a lack of motivation, and a lack of the necessary skills or knowledge. Knowing and understanding these factors can help individuals and organizations take the necessary steps to avoid delays in success.

POSSIBLE DIFFICULTIES WITH ACHIEVING SUCCESS

1.

Achieving success is not always easy. There are a number of potential difficulties that may arise, which can make success difficult to attain.

The first difficulty is the lack of motivation. Without a clear goal or vision, it can be difficult to stay motivated and continue to strive for success. Having a plan and taking actionable steps towards success can help to keep an individual motivated.

Another difficulty is the fear of failure. It can be difficult to take risks and push for success if there is a fear of failure. It is important to remember that failure is a part of the learning process and can help to open up new opportunities.

Thirdly, there can be a lack of resources available. This can be a particular issue if an individual is starting out in business. Without access to financial resources, it can be difficult to find the right people and resources to help achieve success.

Finally, competition can be a challenge. With a crowded marketplace, it can be difficult to stand out and make a name for oneself. It is important to stay focused on the goal and to work hard to gain and maintain a competitive advantage.

In conclusion, there are numerous possible difficulties with achieving success. It is important to remain motivated and take risks, while also being aware of the potential lack of resources and competition that may arise. With the right attitude and hard work, success is achievable.

2.

Achieving success can be a difficult endeavor. It often requires an individual to have a clear understanding of their goals, the resources and capabilities to reach those goals, and the determination to put in the hard work and dedication necessary to get there. Additionally, there are a variety of external factors that can make success harder to obtain.

One of the main difficulties in achieving success is the lack of a clear vision or plan. Without a specific goal in mind, it is almost impossible to work towards a desired outcome. To make progress, it is essential to have a well-defined plan of action and a clear understanding of what it takes to reach the ultimate goal.

Time management is another key challenge to achieving success.

With limited resources, it is important to prioritize tasks and use available time as efficiently as possible. It requires discipline to focus on the most important tasks and to make sure they are completed in a timely manner.

A third difficulty in achieving success is the presence of personal and external limitations. These can include an individual's lack of skills and knowledge, or environmental factors such as limited funds or access to resources. In addition, it can be difficult to stay motivated and to remain focused on the goal when faced with these limitations.

Finally, success is often blocked by the presence of fear and doubt. It can be difficult to take risks and make decisions that are necessary for progress when fear and doubt are present. To be successful, it is important to have the courage to take risks and to be able to trust in one's own abilities and decisions.

In conclusion, there are many potential difficulties that can stand in the way of achieving success. It is important to have a clear understanding of one's goals, to prioritize tasks, to recognize and work to overcome personal and external limitations, and to stay motivated and brave in the face of fear and doubt. With the right mindset and dedication, success can be achieved.

3.

Achieving success is no easy feat, and many people face difficulties along the way. One of the first difficulties one may encounter is fear. Fear of failure or not being good enough can prevent a person from attempting to succeed. It can be difficult to find the motivation to keep pushing forward when fear is present.

Another possible difficulty one may face is a lack of resources. Many people don't have access to the same resources that others may have. This can lead to feelings of inadequacy and can be a major roadblock in achieving success.

Other difficulties can come in the form of criticism. Criticism from family, friends, or society can be difficult to handle. It can be discouraging when one is trying to make progress and is met with criticism. It can be tempting to give up and quit, rather than push forward in the face of criticism.

Finally, one may struggle with a lack of discipline. Many people may have a hard time staying focused and devoted to their goals. It can be difficult to stay on track and maintain a consistent effort. Without the proper discipline, it can be hard to make progress and reach success.

Overall, achieving success can be a challenging journey. Fear, lack of resources, criticism, and a lack of discipline can all contribute to difficulties along the way. It is important to stay focused and determined in order to reach success despite any obstacles that may arise.

HOW SUCCESS GROW

1.

Successful growth is a process that many businesses strive to achieve. It involves making the right decisions at the right time in order to increase revenue, profits and customer base. It can be achieved through a combination of strategic planning, effective marketing, and product or service delivery.

The first step to successful growth is strategic planning. This involves setting long-term goals and objectives for the business, and developing a plan to achieve them. It includes analyzing the market, researching competitors, and assessing the business's current strengths and weaknesses. Strategic planning also involves setting short-term goals, such as increasing sales or customer satisfaction, and identifying ways to reach them.

Effective marketing is an important part of successful growth. This involves researching customer needs and wants, developing effective promotional campaigns, and using various media to reach potential customers. It also involves using analytics to track customer behavior and measure the success of marketing campaigns.

Product or service delivery is also a key element of successful growth. This involves creating a product or service that meets customer expectations, delivering it on time and within budget, and providing excellent customer service. It also involves using modern technology to streamline processes and increase efficiency.

Finally, successful growth requires continuous improvement. This involves continuously monitoring the market and customer feedback, assessing the effectiveness of current strategies, and making changes as needed. It also involves developing new products and services, and implementing new technologies to ensure that the business remains competitive.

Successful growth is an ongoing process. It involves making the right decisions at the right time and utilizing the right strategies to ensure that the business is able to grow and remain competitive. By following a strategic plan, implementing effective marketing campaigns, delivering a quality product or service, and continuously improving, businesses can create a successful and sustainable growth plan.

2.

Success is something that everyone strives for and works to achieve. It's a journey filled with hard work, dedication, and perseverance in order to reach a certain level of success. There is no one-size-fits-all approach to achieving success, and it will look different for each individual. However, there are certain elements that will help foster and sustain success.

One key element of success is having a clear vision. You need to have a clear understanding of what success looks like for you in order to be able to achieve it. This requires setting goals and having a plan of action to reach those goals. When you have a clear vision of where you want to be, you can then focus your efforts on getting there.

Another key element of success is taking action. You need to take consistent, meaningful action in order to reach your goals. This means having the discipline to stay focused on the task at hand and to not let distractions get in the way. It also means being able to take risks, as this can lead to greater rewards.

Having a support system is also an important factor in achieving success. It's important to have people who support you and can help you stay on track. This could include friends, family, mentors, or colleagues. Having someone to motivate you and cheer you on when times get tough can make a huge difference in your ability to reach success.

Finally, resilience is a key factor in achieving success. No matter how many times you fail, you need to keep pushing forward. Success isn't a straight line, and there will be plenty of bumps along the way. Being able to pick yourself up and keep going is essential to reaching your goals.

Success is a journey, and there are many components that go into achieving it. Having a clear vision, taking action, having a support system, and being resilient are just a few of the elements that will help foster and sustain success. With dedication and perseverance, success is attainable

3.

Success is an incredibly important concept in all areas of life. It can mean different things to different people, but there are some common elements that can be applied to any situation. In order to understand how success grows, it is important to look at the various factors that contribute to it.

First and foremost, it is important to recognize that hard work and dedication are the most important components of success. By setting goals and taking action to reach those goals, it is possible to achieve success. This requires a great deal of commitment, discipline, and focus. It is also important to remember that failure is a part of the process. Learning to accept setbacks and try again is an important part of the journey.

It is also important to remember that the journey to success takes time. Achieving success requires patience, consistency, and dedication. It is important to stay focused on the goals, and to persist in the face of obstacles. Additionally, it is important to recognize that failure is part of the process and to use it as an opportunity to learn and grow.

One of the key elements of successful growth is networking. By building relationships with other people in the same field, it is possible to increase access to resources and increase one's knowledge base. Networking can also lead to collaboration, which can be beneficial for both parties.

Finally, it is important to recognize that success is not a destination, but a journey. It is important to focus on the process and to constantly strive for self-improvement. By setting short-term and long-term goals, it is possible to stay motivated and make incremental progress. With dedication and perseverance, it is possible to achieve success.

4.

Success is a multifaceted concept that can mean different things to different people. It is something that is not easily defined and is often personal to the individual. However, regardless of the individual's definition, success can be achieved and grown. To do so, it is important to have a plan and a willingness to take risks.

The first step to achieving success is to set goals. Goals provide direction and purpose, helping to focus one's efforts towards a desired outcome. Goals will also provide a measure of success, allowing the individual to track progress and adjust the plan accordingly. When setting goals, it is important to challenge oneself yet remain realistic. Unrealistic goals can lead to frustration and disappointment, while goals that are too easy can lead to complacency.

The second step to success is to take risks. Taking risks can be uncomfortable and intimidating, but it is often necessary to achieve success. Taking risks can lead to great rewards, such as the opportunity to learn new skills, gain experience, and earn recognition. It is important to weigh the risks and rewards before taking a risk.

The third step to success is to stay focused on the goal. Even with a plan and a willingness to take risks, success can be elusive. The individual must stay focused on the goal and maintain a consistent effort. It is important to stay motivated and make adjustments to the plan if needed.

The fourth step to success is to stay organized. Having a plan is important, but it is also important to stay organized. It is important to prioritize tasks and make sure that all tasks are completed on time.

Staying organized can help to minimize distractions and keep the individual on track.

Finally, the fifth step to success is to stay positive and celebrate successes. Celebrating successes, no matter how small, can help to motivate and maintain a positive attitude. Staying positive can help to foster a growth mindset, which will help to encourage further success.

Success can be achieved and grown with a plan, a willingness to take risks, staying focused on the goal, staying organized, and staying positive. When working towards success, it is important to challenge oneself but remain realistic, weigh the risks and rewards, stay motivated, and celebrate successes. With a good plan and the right attitude, success can be attained.

HOW TO KEEP/MAINTAIN SUCCESS

1.

Success is something that is achieved through dedication, hard work, and determination. It requires both short-term and long-term strategies. Here are some tips to help you maintain success:

1. Establish Goals: By setting realistic and achievable goals, you can measure and track your

progress. Setting goals helps to give you focus, direction, and motivation. It also helps you to stay organized and on track.

2. Prioritize: Prioritizing tasks helps to ensure that your efforts are spent on the most important tasks. This helps to ensure that you stay on track and do not get bogged down in unnecessary tasks.

3. Stay Organized: Staying organized is key to success. It helps you to stay on track and save time. Make sure to keep all of

your tasks, documents, and notes organized so that you can easily access them when needed.

4. Take Time for Yourself: Balance is essential for success. Taking time for yourself is important for maintaining a positive mindset and staying focused. Make sure to take regular breaks and allocate time for self-care.

5. Measure Results: Measuring and tracking your progress is key to understanding how to improve your efforts. It helps you to stay on

track and adjust your strategy if needed.

6. Surround Yourself with Positive People: Surrounding yourself with positive and supportive people can help to keep you motivated and inspired. It also helps to create an atmosphere of success.

7. Celebrate Your Successes: Celebrating small successes can help to keep you motivated to achieve your goals. Celebrating successes also helps to recognize your efforts and hard work.

By following these tips, you can maintain success and reach your goals. Setting goals, prioritizing tasks, staying organized, taking time for yourself, measuring results, surrounding yourself with positive people, and celebrating successes are key to success and should be part of your strategy.

2.

Success is highly sought after and desired by many, yet it is not always a simple endeavor. It requires dedication, hard work, and perseverance, as well as a commitment to never give up. To maintain success, there are a few key steps that must be taken.

First, it is important to set and maintain clear goals. Having a plan of action and a specific target to strive for will help keep you on track and motivated. Without goals, it is easy to get sidetracked and lose focus. Setting long-term and short-term goals can help keep you on track and focused on achieving success.

Second, it is essential to stay organized. Organization can be a key factor in productivity and success. Having a plan for how to achieve your goals, including what tasks need to be completed and when, can prevent you from wasting valuable time and resources.

Third, it is important to stay dedicated and motivated. Dedication and motivation are essential ingredients of successful people. Working hard and never giving up can be the difference between success and failure. It is important to stay focused on the goal and never lose sight of what you are trying to accomplish.

Fourth, it is important to stay open to new ideas and experiences. Successful people are willing to take risks and try new things. They are not afraid to think outside the box and explore new possibilities. This can be a great way to open up new opportunities and explore new horizons.

Finally, it is important to stay humble and remember to give back. Successful people are often those who are most generous. They take the time to help others and give back to the community. This can be a great way to stay connected with other successful people and to remain humble and focused on helping others.

Success is not always easy and maintaining success is an ongoing effort. However, by following these steps and remaining dedicated, organized and motivated, success can be achieved.

3.

Success is something that many of us strive for, and it is important to understand how to keep it. There are several key steps to take in order to maintain success.

The first step is to set goals and to stay focused on them. Having a clear goal or set of goals will help to keep you motivated and on track. It is important to set realistic, achievable goals that are measurable. That way, you can track your progress and make adjustments as needed.

The second step is to develop a plan. A plan should be created that outlines how the goals are to be achieved. This plan should be detailed, including tasks, deadlines and the resources needed to accomplish each task. This plan should be reviewed regularly to ensure that it is being followed and that the tasks are being completed on time.

The third step is to take action. After creating a plan, it is important to take action and put it into practice. All of the goals and tasks that have been outlined need to be completed in order to achieve success. Taking action means taking the necessary steps to meet the goals that have been set.

The fourth step is to stay motivated. It is important to stay motivated and to keep pushing forward. This can be done by setting small goals that can be achieved quickly and by rewarding yourself when goals are met. It is also important to stay positive and to stay focused on the end goal.

The fifth step is to be persistent. It is likely that there will be times when progress is slow or when obstacles or challenges arise. It is important to stay persistent and to continue to take action and make progress even when things are not going as planned.

Finally, it is important to measure progress. It is important to track progress and to measure success.

This can be done by setting milestones and tracking progress each step of the way. Measuring progress will help to identify any areas that may need improvement and to ensure that goals are being met.

By following these steps, it is possible to maintain success. Setting goals, developing a plan, taking action, staying motivated, being persistent and measuring progress are all important steps to take. This will help to ensure that success is achieved and maintained.

4.

Maintaining success is an ongoing process that involves focus, commitment, and continual improvement. Here are five key steps to help you keep your success:

1. Set Goals: Goals provide direction and focus, and offer a sense of accomplishment when achieved. Set short-term goals that are achievable and are within your control. It's also important to set long-term goals that are challenging yet realistic.

2. Monitor Your Progress: Evaluate your progress regularly. Celebrate your successes, but also pay attention to areas where you can improve. This will ensure that your goals remain realistic and achievable.

3. Remain Focused: Focus is key in achieving success. Avoid distractions that can take away from your goal. Stay organized and break down tasks into achievable steps.

4. Seek Opportunities: Always be on the lookout for opportunities to further your success. This could include attending seminars, taking classes, or reading books to stay up to date on industry trends and developments.

5. Persevere: When challenges arise, stay motivated and don't give up. Keep a positive attitude and use setbacks as learning experiences. Find ways to stay inspired and focused.

Maintaining success takes time, effort, and dedication. Utilizing these five steps will help you stay on track and stay successful. With focus, commitment, and continual improvement, you can achieve your goals and maintain your success.

HOW TIME AFFECT SUCCESS

1.

Time is an essential factor when it comes to success. It is impossible to achieve success without managing and utilizing one's time effectively. Time can be seen as a tool that can be used to help reach desired goals, or it can be wasted away, leading to the lack of success.

Time affects success in a number of ways. Firstly, time management is essential to being successful. It is important to plan and allocate time to tasks, such as completing assignments, studying, and working, in order to meet deadlines and reach goals. Secondly, procrastination can be a major obstacle when it comes to success. Procrastination can lead to missed deadlines and a lack of focus, which can undermine any efforts to be successful. Thirdly, using time wisely can lead to more opportunities. Taking initiative to utilize time for researching, networking, and connecting with professionals and mentors can provide valuable resources and knowledge which can help to reach goals.

Time can also be used to maximize productivity. Allocating time to completing tasks can help to ensure that goals are met and tasks are completed efficiently. It is also important to make sure that enough time is dedicated to personal needs such as self-care and rest, so that the body and mind can stay healthy and energized.

Finally, time can be used to practice and hone skills. Practicing a skill or honing a skill can help to sharpen abilities and perfect them. This can lead to better performance in whatever field one is pursuing.

In conclusion, time is a critical factor in achieving success. Time management, avoiding procrastination, taking initiative to gain more opportunities, maximizing productivity, and honing skills can all help to achieve success. It is essential to manage time wisely and use it to its full potential in order to achieve success.

2.

Time is a powerful factor in determining success. It can be a great asset or a formidable enemy, depending on how it is used. On one hand, taking the necessary time to plan and execute a task can lead to great success. Taking the time to research and analyze can help to ensure that the necessary steps are taken to achieve one's goals. On the other hand, procrastination and lack of planning can lead to a lack of success.

Time can be used to generate momentum in order to reach a goal. Allocating time to a goal and taking consistent steps towards it will ensure that progress is made. For example, if one wants to learn a new skill, setting aside an hour or two a day to practice and study can help to make steady progress.

Making sure that these allocated hours are used for the task at hand and not wasted on other activities is key to achieving success.

Time can also be used to rest and recharge.Takingthetimefor self-care is important to ensure that one has the energy and enthusiasm to keep going. Taking breaks from work, getting enough sleep and eating a balanced diet can help to maintain focus and energy.

Time can be used to reflect and review. Taking the time to review and reflect on what has been done and what can be done better can help to identify areas of improvement. Taking the time to reflect on the progress being made and make adjustments can help to stay on track and reach the desired goal.

In conclusion, time is a critical factor in success. Taking the time to plan, set aside dedicated hours to work, rest and reflect can help to ensure that the desired goals are achieved. Using time wise and efficiently can be the difference between success and failure.

3.

Time is an integral component of success. Whether we realize it or not, time has an immense influence on the opportunities we have and our ability to capitalize on them. It's important to recognize that time affects success in many ways, and that understanding this can help us make better decisions and be more successful.

First and foremost, time is a crucial factor when it comes to our ability to take advantage of opportunities. Opportunities come and go in life, and being able to capitalize on the right ones when they arise is an important part of success. Having the time to recognize the potential of an opportunity and act on it is essential. If you don't have the time to recognize, analyze, and act on an opportunity when it arises, you may miss out on the chance to capitalize on it.

Second, time is an important factor when it comes to developing skills and knowledge. Successful people are often those who have taken the time to develop the skills and knowledge necessary to succeed in their chosen fields. Taking the time to learn and practice new skills can be the difference between success and failure. Without the time to research and study, we may not be able to develop the necessary skills to reach our goals.

Third, the amount of time you spend on a task or goal can have a significant impact on your success. If you spend too much time on a task or goal, you may not have the time to move on to the next task or goal. On the other hand, if you don't spend enough time on a task or goal, you may not be able to complete it properly or reach your desired results. Finding the right balance between the time spent on a task and the time spent on other tasks is essential for success.

Finally, time can be a great motivator. Having a deadline to work towards can help us stay focused and motivated to complete our tasks and goals. Knowing that we have a limited amount of time to complete a task or reach a goal can help us stay on track and keep us from procrastinating or giving up.

Time is an essential element of success. Understanding the ways in which time affects success can help us make better decisions and be more successful. Taking the time to develop the necessary skills, recognizing and taking advantage of opportunities when they arise, and finding the right balance between the time spent on tasks can help us achieve our goals.

4.

Time is an important factor in achieving success in any endeavor. It has the ability to help or hinder progress and should be managed carefully to ensure the best possible outcome.

Time can be a great ally in the pursuit of success. It allows us to plan, organize and set goals to ensure that our efforts are directed towards the desired outcome. If we use our time wisely, we can maximize our productivity and increase our chances of success. On the other hand, if we do not manage our time well, it can become a hindrance, wasting valuable energy and effort.

Time can also affect our mindset. When we have a limited amount of time to complete something, it can create stress and anxiety. This can lead to rushed decisions and poor performance. However, when we have ample time to prepare and plan, it can help us to stay focused and motivated, leading to better outcomes.

Time is a valuable commodity and should be used wisely. When striving for success, it is important to plan, prioritize and set realistic goals. This will ensure that we use our time efficiently and effectively, giving us the best opportunity of achieving our desired outcome.

5.

Time is an integral factor in achieving success. It affects success in myriad ways, both directly and indirectly. One of the most obvious ways time affects success is by providing the opportunity to work hard and smart. The more time you have, the more opportunities you have to work for success. Additionally, time allows for more strategic planning, as you have the opportunity to plan out your goals and how to reach them. Additionally, there is the factor of patience, which is essential for success. Time allows you to wait for the right moment to take action and to recognize the right opportunities.

Time also affects success through the ability to learn and grow. With a longer time frame, you can take advantage of more learning opportunities, from formal education to trial and error, which will ultimately help you achieve success. Similarly, time gives you the opportunity to grow and develop necessary skills. You have the opportunity to practice and hone your skills and knowledge, which can help you in achieving success.

Time also affects success through the ability to build relationships. Success often relies on the relationships that you build, as it is often through these relationships that you gain access to the right people and resources. With time, you have the opportunity to build and nurture relationships with the right people and organizations, which can be invaluable resources in achieving success.

Finally, time affects success through the factor of luck. While luck plays a role in success, time increases the chances of luck playing a role in success. With more time, you have more opportunities to take advantage of favorable circumstances and situations, which can be key to achieving success.

Overall, it is clear that time plays a critical role in success. Time provides more opportunity, more learning and growth, more chances to build relationships, and more chances to take advantage of luck. All of these factors are important in achieving success and time is essential in allowing them to take place.

www.ingramcontent.com/pod-product-compliance
Lightning Source LLC
Chambersburg PA
CBHW081516220526
45467CB00010B/2943